# EVERYTHING YOU NEED TO KNOW ABOUT COMMAS

## GIACOMO GIAMMATTEO

INFERNO PUBLISHING COMPANY

# TITLE PAGE

GIACOMO GIAMMATTEO
INFERNO PUBLISHING COMPANY"

© **2021** Giacomo Giammatteo. All rights reserved. No part of this book may be reproduced or transmitted in any form or by any means, electronic or mechanical, including photocopying, recording, or by any information storage and retrieval system, without written permission from the author, except for the inclusion of brief quotations in a review.

Inferno Publishing Company

Houston, TX

For more information about this book, visit my website.

**Edition ISBNs**

**Trade Hardback** 978-1-949074-64-2

**E-book** 978-1-949074-63-5

**Cover design by Natasha Brown**

**Book design by Giacomo Giammatteo**

**This edition was prepared by Giacomo Giammatteo gg@giacomog.com**

❦ Created with Vellum

# INTRODUCTION
## INTRODUCTION

One note about commas before we begin. Commas are often used to indicate a pause or break between the different parts of a sentence. Above all else, they are meant to clarify or make the meaning more clear. They do this in various ways: they separate items in a list, offset the nonessential parts of a sentence, mark a pause following an introductory clause or word, and note who is being spoken to when using dialogue.

The main thing to understand is that commas are not inserted arbitrarily; the rules regarding when and how to use them exist to enhance clarity—no other reason.

With that said, let's delve into the rules.

# EVERYTHING YOU NEED TO KNOW ABOUT COMMAS

*I*f you've written more than an occasional email or letter to a relative, you have undoubtedly had concerns regarding the proper placement of commas. If you write professionally, those concerns should be at the forefront of your worries. Professional writers *should* use editors, but even so, they often do writing that doesn't see the editor's eye—things like blogs, query letters, proposals, outlines, and anything subject to social media scrutiny. That's one reason why it is so important to learn as much as you can—to maintain a professional appearance at all times.

I can't guarantee this book will answer *all* your questions regarding commas, but it should take care of most. First, we'll cover the basics, then we'll move on to specific examples. Some of the basics as well as a few of the specifics were in my book *Simply Put: The Plain English Grammar Guide*. The rest I've added to make a more comprehensive reference.

# WHAT ARE COMMAS USED FOR?

*A*ccording to the *Oxford English Dictionary*:

A comma marks a slight break between different parts of a sentence. Used properly, commas make the meaning of sentences clear by grouping and separating words, phrases, and clauses. Many people are uncertain about the use of commas and often sprinkle them throughout their writing without knowing the basic rules.

Here are the main cases when you need to use a comma:

• in lists of three or more items

• in direct speech

• to separate clauses

• to set off certain parts of a sentence

• with *however* and other conjunctions (connecting words)

There are a lot of rules governing the use of commas, and some can be confusing. The rules dealing with lists and dialogue are fairly rigid, but they are also simple to understand. The separation of clauses is more complex. I've tried to list the more confusing ones below, and I explain them in plain language instead of using grammatical terms so that anyone can understand how it's done.

I sometimes think that dictionaries and grammarians are associated with the legal and insurance professions; they continually try to complicate things with obscure language.

USE A COMMA AFTER A DEPENDENT CLAUSE THAT STARTS A SENTENCE

*I* told you I wouldn't resort to grammatical terms, so let's dumb it down. A "dependent clause" is no different than a dependent child; they both rely on something or someone else for support. A dependent child relies on their parents or guardians, and a dependent clause relies on the rest of the sentence for support; in other words, it doesn't make sense by itself. Let's look at a few examples:

- When I went to the bank, (dependent clause)

- When I took a walk, (dependent clause)

- After driving to the city, (dependent clause)

All the above are dependent clauses and require more substance to complete the sentence. Examples are below:

- When I went to the bank, I made a deposit. (complete sentence)

- When I took a walk, I got robbed. (complete sentence)

• After driving to the city, I lay down and napped. (complete sentence)

If you switch the order of the sentence, the comma is no longer needed. Let's take a look.

• I made a deposit when I went to the bank.

• I got robbed when I took a walk.

• I lay down for a nap after driving to the city.

That took a lot of explaining for one simple rule, but I like to use examples because I think people understand them better.

# USE A COMMA BEFORE A COORDINATING CONJUNCTION THAT CONNECTS TWO INDEPENDENT CLAUSES

That rule is rife with grammatical terms, so let's break it down.

A "coordinating conjunction" is a word that connects. In this case, it connects two "independent clauses," which means they could be stand-alone sentences. Let's look at a few examples.

**PS:** From now on, when I refer to a "connecting word," it means a conjunction of some sort; after all, a conjunction connects.

☑ I went to the bank, and I made a deposit.

☑ I took a walk, and I got robbed.

In both sentences, each part of the sentence on either side of the connecting word *and* could be its own sentence.

- I went to the bank.

- I made a deposit.

If you remove the subject (I) from the second part, though, it changes everything because that sentence can no longer stand on its own, which means you no longer need a comma to separate them.

☑ I went to the bank and made a deposit.

☑ I took a walk and got robbed.

Don't let the complexity of a sentence fool you either. Look at the following example.

• She took a walk instead of a jog, and she got lost on her way home.

If you break that down, it's no different than the sentences above. Take a look.

• She took a walk instead of a jog.

• She got lost on her way home.

The main coordinating conjunctions (connecting words) are easy to remember if you use the acronym FANBOYS. It stands for *for, and, nor, but, or, yet,* and *so.*

There are other types of conjunctions (or connecting words), but we'll get to them at another time.

# USE A COMMA TO SEPARATE ITEMS IN A LIST OF THREE OR MORE

This rule applies when you have three or more items. In the following sentence, only two items are mentioned, so you don't need a comma to separate them.

✗ I went to the bank to make a deposit, and get a withdrawal. (two items)

✓ I went to the bank to make a deposit, get a withdrawal, and open a new account. (three items)

✗ The sandwiches I like are turkey, and peanut butter.

✓ The sandwiches I like are turkey, peanut butter, and tomato with cheese.

You'll need to be careful when using commas with lists. There is still a controversy regarding the use of the final comma, which is referred to as the "Oxford" comma. Some people swear by it, while others claim it is not needed.

The Oxford comma is suggested for a reason: to clear up ambiguity. Take the last sentence and look at it both ways.

☑ The sandwiches I like are turkey, peanut butter, and tomato with cheese.

✗ The sandwiches I like are turkey, peanut butter and tomato with cheese.

Although I doubt this would confuse anyone, it could. Taken at face value, the sentence could mean you like turkey sandwiches as well as peanut-butter-and-tomato sandwiches with cheese.

I am a proponent of the Oxford comma, and if you want to be understood clearly, I suggest you follow suit.

I'll give one more example. One of my favorite movies is an old western featuring Clint Eastwood. The title is *The Good, the Bad and the Ugly*. And it's punctuated exactly that way, with no comma after *bad*.

However, when I say it, and when I hear others pronounce the name, there is a definite pause after *bad*, as if a comma belongs there. In fact, the Italian name for the movie (it was made in Italy) is *Il Buono, il Brutto, il Cattivo*.

As you can see, there are commas after each adjective. I think it sounds better that way.

Besides, if you don't use a comma, it could be interpreted as being about two people: the good, and the bad and ugly. With the comma, it leaves no doubt: it's about three people—the good, the bad, and the ugly.

## USE A COMMA TO OFFSET NONESSENTIAL INFORMATION

I'll simplify this. If you have a phrase or part of a sentence that is merely there to provide additional information, use a comma to offset it.

Use a comma before it if it completes the sentence and on each side of it if it falls in the middle of the sentence. Examples follow:

☑ I went to the bank and saw Jane, one of the tellers.

☑ I went to the bank and saw Jane, one of the tellers, as she got out of the cab.

In each case, the phrase offset by the comma was not needed.

☑ I went to the bank and saw Jane.

☑ I went to the bank and saw Jane as she got out of the cab.

As you can see, when we removed "one of the tellers" from each sentence, it was still a complete sentence, and the meaning didn't change. "One of the tellers" was simply additional information about Jane.

If the word or phrase is necessary, though, do *not* use a comma. Here are a couple of sentences showing the difference.

☑ My niece Bella calls me almost every night.

☑ My wife, Mikki, fixes my coffee every day.

In the first sentence, we didn't use a comma because *Bella* is a necessary part of the sentence. I needed to mention her name to distinguish her from the other nieces I have. If I had just said, "My niece calls me almost every night," you wouldn't know which niece calls.

In the second sentence, however, *Mikki* is not needed because I have only one wife. There is no need to mention her name.

Nonessential clauses (phrases) are one of the more common reasons to insert commas. They aren't always easy to recognize, but if you remove the questionable clause, and if the sentence still retains the same meaning, then it is nonessential.

# USE A COMMA TO OFFSET A NEGATIVE COMMENT IN OPPOSITION TO THE SENTENCE, AND USE IT WHETHER IT OCCURS MIDSENTENCE OR AT THE END

- *I* went to the bank, not the restaurant.
- I stopped at the restaurant, not the bank, so I have no money.
- He's a nice guy, not mean but sweet.
- He's a nice guy, not mean.
- She wanted to go to the movies, not the opera.
- I voted for the opera, not the movies, and I'll bet you can guess where we ended up going.

# PLACE A COMMA BETWEEN ADJECTIVES THAT MODIFY THE SAME NOUN

It will be easier to show this with examples.

- Mollie was a pretty mean dog.
- The bear that attacked was a big, furry bear.
- She lived in a big, expensive house.

Sometimes several adjectives are used before a noun but don't modify the noun the same way. If they modify the noun independently, put a comma between them.

There are several ways you can tell whether or not to use a comma. The first is to place the word *and* between the adjectives and see if the sentence still makes sense. Let's take the sentences above and test it.

- Mollie was a pretty and mean dog.
- The bear that attacked was a big *and* furry bear.
- She lived in a big *and* expensive house.

Sentence number one changes meaning. Mollie goes from being considered "pretty mean" (somewhat mean) to being thought of as *pretty* and *mean*.

Sentences two and three sound fine. "It was a big and furry bear" and "She lived in a big and expensive house." Neither of those sentences is ideal as far as I'm concerned, but they work.

The second way to determine what and how the adjectives modify the noun is to rearrange them.

- Mollie was a mean pretty dog.
- The bear that attacked was a furry, big bear.
- She lived in an expensive, big house.

Now, look at each sentence and how rearranging the adjectives affected the meaning. In sentence one, it now reads "Mollie was a mean pretty dog," meaning Mollie was a pretty dog that was mean. That's different than the original. In the original, it said Mollie was mean, but it didn't imply she was pretty.

Sentences two and three don't change in meaning.

# WHEN A TITLE FOLLOWS A NAME, USE COMMAS TO SEPARATE IT FROM THE REST OF THE SENTENCE

*A*gain, examples show it best.

- Donald Trump, the president, is disliked by many people.

- Sean McGonigle, the chief of police, was reappointed by the mayor.

- The governor, Jasper Jenkins, will be in attendance.

- Janet Ringlar, senator from Arizona, will speak at the ceremony.

This even applies to degrees if listed. See the examples below.

- Mary Simpson, PhD (or Ph.D.), will speak at the dinner reception.

- Johnathan Manns, MBA, will speak after her.

# USE COMMAS TO SEPARATE THE MONTH AND DAY FROM THE YEAR IN A DATE AND TO SEPARATE THE STREET ADDRESS, CITY, AND STATE IN AN ADDRESS

This is a fairly straightforward rule, but even so, examples follow:

- My grandson was born on April 21, 2015.

- Sean lives at 555 Orange Street, Austin, TX 78617.

If only the month and year are used, no comma is necessary. Commas are necessary for separation of city and state, though.

- My grandson was born in April 2015

- She lives in San Francisco, CA.

# USE COMMAS TO SEPARATE NUMBERS OF FOUR DIGITS OR MORE

*M*ost everyone knows this, but we'll give examples just in case.

- 36,577

- 1,998

- 124,222

- 2,467,655

One more note about commas with numbers:

if you are writing metric measurements, use spaces instead of commas. This will avoid confusion for European readers who are accustomed to seeing commas used as decimal points.

- He bought a 16,7 hectare farm in Tuscany. (European way)

- He bought a 16.7 hectare farm in Tuscany. (U.S. way)

- They needed a minimum of 2 449 hectares for the resort. (A space instead of a comma)

If we had used a comma and not a space in the last example, a person used to seeing commas used as decimal points would have read that as "2.449" hectares (quite a difference).

# USE A COMMA AFTER AN ADVERB THAT INTRODUCES A CLAUSE

Here are a few example sentences:

- Inadvertently, I spilled the wine.
- Finally, he caught the killer.
- Mistakenly, he locked her up.

Many guides make exceptions for one-word introductions where clarity is not affected. The words *now*, *nowadays*, *today*, and *yesterday* are some of the words allowed exceptions.

- Yesterday we went to the zoo.

You could use a comma after *yesterday*, but you don't have to. Either is fine. Here are more examples:

- Now is the time to go.
- Nowadays everyone has a cell phone.
- Yesterday was the perfect weather for swimming.

- Today won't be ideal for baseball or soccer.

This is one of those "rules" that would benefit by using the "place a comma when you hear a pause" guide. It is a stylistic choice and often depends on where the writer wants emphasis.

# USE A COMMA AFTER A CONJUNCTIVE (CONNECTING) ADVERB THAT LINKS/CONNECTS TWO INDEPENDENT CLAUSES

*E*xamples:

- My sister got carded at the store; therefore, we got no wine.

- My dog isn't very big; however, he scared off the intruder.

- She studied hard for the test; consequently, she got an A.

If the situation does not call for a semicolon, use commas on either side of the conjunctive adverb (connecting word).

- He didn't believe, however, that money was a factor.

In the last example, "that money was a factor" is not an independent clause.

Below is a list to use as a reference.

**LIST OF CONJUNCTIVE ADVERBS**

- accordingly

- additionally
- also
- besides
- comparatively
- consequently
- conversely
- elsewhere
- equally
- finally
- further
- furthermore
- hence
- henceforth
- however
- in addition
- in comparison
- in contrast
- indeed
- instead
- likewise
- meanwhile
- moreover

- namely
- nevertheless
- next
- nonetheless
- now
- otherwise
- rather
- similarly
- still
- subsequently
- then
- thereafter
- therefore
- thus
- yet

# USE COMMAS WHEN ATTRIBUTING QUOTES

Whether you're writing novels or nonfiction, you will invariably come across the need to use a direct quote, and when you do, you'll need a comma to offset that quote. The examples below show how.

- "I'm not staying," Joe said. "I'll be leaving after dinner."

- Margaret glared and said, "Why not?"

- "I'm going to the mall, Mom," Jenny said.

- Jenny said, "I'm going to the mall, Mom."

# USE A COMMA AFTER YES AND NO WHEN THEY OCCUR AT THE BEGINNING OF A SENTENCE

Take a look at the two examples below:

- *Yes*, I'm going to the bank.
- *No*, I won't be making a deposit while I'm there.

There are other words (interjections) that need commas after them as well. Below are a few that occur at the beginning of a sentence, but often, interjections need commas before and after them when they occur midsentence.

- Well, I'm shocked at his response.
- Oh, I don't care if we go or not.
- Shh, the baby's sleeping.

Interjections midsentence.

- She put on her new nightgown, and, wow, did she look great!
- I don't really like him, but, well, he *is* rich.

Many writers use all the tools available to them, so instead of using commas in instances such as these, they opt for em dashes. Let's look.

• She put on her new nightgown, and—wow—did she look great!

Most people believe the second construction, the one using the em dash, adds more punch to the sentence, so if that's what you're after, use it.

There are cases where the comma after *yes* or *no* may be omitted. One such case is shown below. Imagine a teenager talking with their mother.

"I can go to the mall if I want."

"No you can't! And don't dare try."

# USE A COMMA WHEN DIRECTLY ADDRESSING SOMEONE

*A*dditional rules for capitalization apply.

- It's time for us to go, Captain.
- You'll go, Detective, when I say you can go.
- Captain, it's not right to hold us back.

This doesn't cover every instance where you need a comma, but it covers most. Even a professional writer may go years without encountering a circumstance not mentioned here.

At the end of the next chapter, we cover examples of how and when to use commas with specific words and phrases.

# RULES ARE NOT RULES

*L*ike everything else, there are rules that govern punctuation with dialogue tags. It just so happens that one of them I don't agree with.

There aren't many times I don't listen to my editors, but there are a few. I don't mean the odd occurrence when an editor makes a call on whether to capitalize a word or something like that. I'm talking about repeated usage contrary to the *rules* of writing.

I'm going to discuss one of those rules. It deals with the use of commas. But before we do that, let's take a look at some other rules governing comma usage with specific words.

I know we just spent a lot of time learning about commas, but they can be tricky, so it may be worthwhile to review some of the rules. If you don't think you need to go over them, skip this part.

# COMMAS WITH CERTAIN WORDS

*A* while ago, I promised to address the issues people often face when using commas with certain words and phrases. The next few chapters don't cover them all, but they deal with a few of the more confusing ones.

Knowing when and how to use commas is one of the more challenging aspects of punctuation.

Periods, question marks, exclamation points, and even the other punctuation marks are easy in comparison.

———————————————

# COMMAS WITH AS

## Commas with *As*

Determining when to use a comma is often difficult, but with the word *as*, it seems even more so.

The meaning of *as* in a sentence is sometimes determined by whether a comma is used.

Consider the following examples:

- He built a fire *as* it was snowing. (while)

- He built a fire, *as* it was snowing. (because)

We have to change the sentence to reflect this, but consider the following:

- He built a fire as it was meant to be. (the way)

Which sentence is correct? All of them. It depends on the intended meaning. Let's analyze them.

- He built a fire *as* it was snowing.

Without a comma, what we're saying is "He built a fire *while* it was snowing."

• He built a fire, *as* it was snowing.

In this example (with the comma), we're saying "He built a fire *because* it was snowing." The *reason* he built a fire was due to the snow.

And in the third example, we're saying he built a fire *the way* it was meant to be.

Let's look at a few more examples.

• He ate lunch *as* the kids were playing. (while)

• He ate lunch, *as* the kids were playing. (because)

• Tina yelled for us to come to dinner *as* the baby was crying. (while)

• Tina yelled for us to come to dinner, *as* the baby was crying. (because)

In the examples above, you can see that when *as* is used in place of *while* or *the way*, there is no comma. But when it's used in place of *because*, it needs a comma.

I hope you have this down pat, but let's look at one more example. See if you can determine what *as* means in each of the following sentences.

• Tony cooked dinner *as* his wife had asked him to.

• Tony cooked dinner, *as* his wife had asked him to.

------------------------

Take a moment and try to work out what *as* means in each of those examples. Both are grammatically correct, but they don't reflect the same meaning.

OKAY, enough time. Let's look at them.

In the first sentence, *as* means "the way." In other words, "Tony cooked dinner *the way* his wife had asked him to."

~

IN THE SECOND SENTENCE, *as* means *because*. "Tony cooked dinner *because* his wife had asked him to."

~

NOTE that if *because* had been used, no comma would have been necessary. "Tony cooked dinner because his wife had asked him to." But we need a comma when *as* is used. With no comma, it leaves a reader to wonder what is meant—*the way* or *because*.

~

THE COMMAS ARE USED for clarity *as* (the way) they should be.

The last thing we need to mention regarding commas with *as* are asides. Asides are short comments used to tell the reader (or, more often, a member of the audience at a play) something that is for their ears only.

These asides can be enclosed within parentheses, offset by em dashes, or surrounded by commas. Commas are often used for shorter asides.

Consider this example. A character is engaged in dialogue with another, and after a fight, the one says to the other, "He's got a hell of a punch, as you can see, and is not a person to be taken lightly.

Two other ways to express this would be the following:

"He's got a hell of a punch—as you can see—and is not a person to be taken lightly.

"He's got a hell of a punch (as you can see) and is not a person to be taken lightly.

There are several other meanings of *as*, but they shouldn't cause confusion because they don't take commas.

*As*—used as "on."

"We bought the house, and we take occupancy as of (on) June 10.

*As*—used as "since".

The deal has been effective as of (since) October 5.

*As*—used as "from."

The deal is effective as of (from) July 12.

*As*—used as "like."

He passed the bar and has been practicing as (like) a lawyer for more than a year.

S OME OTHER EXAMPLES do need commas.

Consider when *as* functions as "for example."

Certain fish, as salt-water fish (for example), need careful tending.

The above construction isn't common, but I've seen it enough that I felt it should be included.

*As well as* is usually fine without a comma, but sometimes, depending on what the writer is trying to convey, a comma is needed. When it is needed, it's almost turning it into an aside, but not quite. Consider the following:

Nick is going to the beach.

Nick and Dana are going to the beach.

Nick, *as well as* Dana, is going to the beach.

You need the commas because it is almost functioning as an aside. It's like saying, "Nick is going to the beach. And, oh yeah, Dana is going too." It's as if it's an afterthought.

One more thing to note is that when this type of construction occurs, it affects the verb as well. The verb remains singular with *as well as*, but if the *as well as* changes to *and*, it requires a plural.

---

AS CAN BE A TRICKY ONE, so carefully analyze what you're trying to say, then decide whether to place a comma.

---

Here are a few sentences with *as* that don't seem to fit the guidelines we've established. Try using the "pause" in your head when you read, though, and I think you'll see it works. I'll list the correct way after you look through them.

- None so blind **as** those who won't see.
- None so deaf **as** those who won't hear.
- When in Rome do **as** the Romans do.
- **As** the life is so is the end.
- Choose an author **as** you choose a friend.
- Nothing so necessary for travelers **as** languages.
- When you are at Rome do **as** Rome does.

- Do in Rome **as** the Romans do.

- Use a book **as** a bee does a flower.

Now, let's look at where the commas go.

- None so blind **as** those who won't see.

- None so deaf **as** those who won't hear.

- When in Rome **(comma needed)**, do **as** the Romans do.

- **As** the life is **(comma needed)**, so is the end.

- Choose an author **as** you choose a friend.

- Nothing so necessary for travelers **as** languages.

- When you are at Rome **(comma needed)**, do **as** Rome does.

- Do in Rome **as** the Romans do.

- Use a book **as** a bee does a flower.

That wraps it up with *as*, so let's move on to *as well as*.

# AS WELL AS

## As Well As

A lot of people pay no attention to commas, and it shows. Commas are critical to reading enjoyment. They instruct readers when to pause or slow down just as other punctuation helps readers know when to get excited or surprised, stop for a long pause, stop and go more quickly, etc.

The key to the proper use of commas is knowing when and how to use them. Many writers seem confused when to use a comma with "as well as."

Many of the "as" phrases—"such as," "as in," "as if," "as though," and more—present a problem. But "as well as" seems to trip people up *as much as*, if not more, than the others.

We'll get to those other phrases in time; for now, let's focus on "as well as."

I did a search using Google's Ngram viewer using "as well as" with and without a comma preceding it or following it. The results showed that people used a comma almost as much as they didn't.

Although the results were surprising, they were understandable. "As well as" is used in situations where it doesn't need a comma, but it is also used where it does require one.

The phrase "as well as" is often used to compare things, such as "She's beautiful *as well as* intelligent."

When it's used like this, it doesn't need a comma, but it's also used in ways that do need a comma.

SHE INSISTED on directing the play and on producing it as well. (equally)

The town grew as well because of its location as because of its superb climate. (as well as, as much or as truly as)

Joan is witty as well as intelligent.

Let's look at the examples provided by a few dictionaries.

• He's brave *as well as* loyal.

• The coach, *as well as* the team, is ready.

• Joan is witty *as well as* intelligent

In the first example, we're saying he's brave *and* loyal. In that case, no comma is needed. The sentence flows (reads well) without a pause.

In the second example, "as well as the team" seems more like an afterthought. It's like saying "The coach is ready. Oh, yeah, the team is too." You could also read it as "The coach is ready *in addition to* the team."

When you have a similar situation—where the person or item mentioned after "as well as" seems like an aside or something less important—you should use a comma.

In the last example, "Joan is pretty as well as intelligent," it seems obvious that "as well as" is used as a conjunction (a connecting word like *and*), and since it is not connecting two independent clauses, no comma is necessary.

Let's look at a few more examples.

- Barbara, *as well as* Tammy, is going to the party.

- Sean and Maddy, *as well as* Nora and Bruce, are going to the beach.

- He doesn't play golf *as well as* his father

In the first and second examples, "as well as" is used to offset two asides, so commas are necessary on both sides of the phrase.

Also note how in the first example, even though we mention Barbara and Tammy, we used a singular verb form while in the example with Sean and Maddy, we used a plural.

The reason is that "as well as" does not make the subject a compound subject, which would require the plural. This only happens in cases where you combine the nouns, in effect, making more than one subject.

- Barbara and Tammy *are* going to the party.

In the above case, there is no aside, simply a conjunction (connecting word) used to create multiple subjects: Barbara *and* Tammy.

In the third example, we state, "He doesn't play golf *as well as* his father." In that sentence, we're using *as well as* to compare. We're comparing how well he plays golf to how well his father plays. No comma is necessary.

**Summary**

That sums it up for "as well as" and comma usage.

🐾 If you are adding a phrase or clause and using it as an aside, use a comma to offset it. And remember, if that phrase falls in the middle of the sentence, it needs commas before and after it (as shown above). If the phrase comes at the end of the sentence, only use a comma preceding it.

🐾 Any other time you use "as well as," no comma is necessary.

------------------------

# BECAUSE

*B*ecause is most often used to connect two clauses in a sentence.

• I went to sleep early because I was tired.

You usually don't need a comma before *because*. An exception is when the clarity of the sentence is at risk. We'll look at when that may happen later.

Regardless of where *because* falls in the sentence, it is introducing a clause that should answer the question *why*.

• Because it was raining, they didn't go swimming. (*Why* didn't they go swimming?)

That is a dependent clause introducing a complete sentence.

• Because it was raining . . . (dependent clause)

• They didn't go swimming. (complete sentence)

In cases where connecting words, such as *because, though, since, etc.*, introduce a complete sentence, a comma follows. Now, let's look at the reverse.

- They didn't go swimming because it was raining. (no comma needed)

- She went to the party because she loved dancing. (no comma) (*Why* did she go to the party?)

When a connecting word introduces a dependent clause following a complete sentence, no comma is needed.

And here comes the exception. You knew there'd be one, didn't you?

As I mentioned earlier, exceptions are made if clarity is at risk. When a sentence begins with a negative, it often muddles the clarity of what follows.

- He didn't win the race because of his ego.

- He didn't win the race, because of his ego.

In the first example (no comma), we're implying he *won* the race but not due to his ego. (It could have been anything else—his natural talent, his physical ability, his determination, etc.)

In the second example (with comma), we're implying he *didn't* win the race, and it was *due to* his ego. (Maybe he hung back too long wanting to show an explosive finish).

- He didn't go for the touchdown because of her.

- He didn't go for the touchdown, because of her.

The same reasoning applies in the above examples.

In the first, he went for the touchdown, but we're implying the reason he went for it had nothing to do with her. In other words, he went for the touchdown for any number of reasons but not because of her. He may have had a bet on the game, maybe he wanted to break a record, or perhaps he simply wanted to win.

- He didn't go for the touchdown because of her; he wanted to break the school record.

In the second example, perhaps he didn't go for the touchdown because she was rooting for the other team (her school) and he didn't want to embarrass her by padding the score.

You should use commas to clarify as much as possible, but it may be simpler to reword the sentence.

- He didn't go for the touchdown because his fiancée was in the stands, rooting for the other team.

Or perhaps there is a more sinister reason he didn't go for the touchdown.

- He didn't go for the touchdown because he was being paid to shave points.

Just remember, you don't use a comma before *because* with the possible exception of when a negative introduces the sentence. In cases like that, it may be simpler to reword the sentence.

We didn't cover *since*, but it is almost interchangeable with *because*, and in examples like the ones we gave, the same rules apply.

---

# WHEN AND WHERE TO USE COMMAS WITH ANYWAY

*Anyway* is often used to mean in spite of (despite) reasons or situations that have already been mentioned. It is also used as another way of saying "regardless." An example follows:

- "I'm going for a walk, dear."
- "But it's raining."
- "I'm going *anyway*."

When *anyway* is used at the end of a sentence (to mean regardless) no comma is necessary. As you'll see later, it isn't needed with *regardless* either.

When *anyway* appears at the beginning of a sentence, it is often being used as a means of "picking up" or "reintroducing" a topic of conversation, whether that occurs informally or in written dialogue. An example follows:

"WE WERE GOING CAMPING, but then the car broke down."

"What happened to it?"

"It was just a flat tire, which we fixed quickly. *Anyway*, after we put the spare on, we continued to the campground."

IN SITUATIONS such as the one above, a comma is placed after *anyway*.

Another example of *anyway* being used to get back on track in a conversation, discussion, argument, etc., follows (especially after going off on a tangent).

SUPPOSE you're writing a mystery novel and the detective is interviewing witnesses. He might ask, "How did you come across the body?"

"I was at the company party, and we all had a few too many, so I decided to call a cab. I waited for almost half an hour, when—"

"The body," the detective said. "How did you discover the body?"

"Oh yeah. *Anyway*, the taxi took us home, and when we walked in the door..."

In informal conversations, *anyway* is often used to express the idea of "at least," but it is seldom seen in formal writing that way.

Anyway, now that we've discussed the word *anyway* so much, let's get back to the topic, which was when to use a comma with *anyway*.

As discussed earlier, when *anyway* comes at the beginning of a sentence, it almost always needs a comma after it. At the beginning of a sentence, it is functioning as an introductory adverb, and as such, needs a comma. On the other hand, when *anyway* comes at the end of a sentence, it rarely needs a comma before it and obviously not after it.

If, however, *anyway* is being used as an adverbial conjunction (conjunctive adverb) to introduce a new clause, a semicolon is usually appropriate before the word with a comma following it. Examples follow:

- It was raining, but I went to the mall anyway. (regardless)

- The forecast didn't call for snow, but we packed our skis and drove to Aspen anyway. (regardless)

- I wanted to go to the prom with Sharon; anyway, I went without her. (conjunctive adverb)

- I got drunk at the Christmas party; anyway, I still got a promotion. (conjunctive adverb)

In the first two examples, *anyway* is used as a synonym for *regardless,* and as such, doesn't need a comma.

In the last two examples (as bad as they are), *anyway* functions as a conjunctive adverb; in other words, an adverb that connects two independent clauses, so it requires a semicolon before it and a comma after it.

Below is a list of conjunctive adverbs. This isn't a complete list, but it represents the most commonly used ones.

## Conjunctive Adverbs

| | | | |
|---|---|---|---|
| accordingly | additionally | also | anyway |
| besides | certainly | comparitively | consequently |
| conversely | elsewhere | equally | finally |
| further | furthermore | hence | henceforth |
| however | in addition | in comparison | in contrast |
| incidentally | indeed | instead | likewise |
| meanwhile | moreover | namely | nevertheless |
| next | nonetheless | now | otherwise |
| rather | similarly | still | subsequently |
| then | thereafter | therefore | thus |
| undoubtedly | Yet | | |

Anyway, let's get back to *anyway*. I'll try to sum it up quickly. To understand how to use commas with *anyway*, follow these rules:

- If it is used as a synonym for *regardless*, you do not need a comma before it.

- If it is being used as a conjunctive adverb, the punctuation required will depend on the position of *anyway* in the sentence. If it is placed after a sentence's initial clause, it requires a semicolon before it, not a comma.

- It does not need a comma before it at the end of a sentence.

- The only time it needs a comma before it is if it comes in between the subject and verb of the sentence, though this would rarely occur outside of written dialogue.

- When *anyway* begins a sentence, a comma is needed after it.

Examples of usage:

- When used as regardless.

- I know it's raining, but I'm going to the beach anyway. (no comma)

- At the beginning of a sentence.

- Anyway, I'll see you when I get there. (comma after)

- As a conjunctive adverb in the middle of a sentence.

I wanted to go to the prom with Sharon; anyway, I went without her. (semicolon before and comma after)

Be careful when *anyway* is used as *regardless* but then has an independent clause following it.

- He told me to do it anyway, so I completed the task.

- He told me to do it anyway; however, I decided not to.

- He told me to do it anyway; consequently, my decision was made.

In each of the above, *anyway* is punctuated as if it was the last word in the sentence; in other words, no comma precedes it. The punctuation that follows it depends on the clause that comes after *anyway*.

We've covered the use of *anyway* when it is used as a synonym for *regardless* (no comma), and we've discussed the punctuation of *anyway* at the beginning of a sentence (comma after it). We've even talked about *anyway* as a conjunctive adverb in the middle of a sentence (no comma before but comma or semicolon after).

Now for the final point. The only time you'll need a comma before it is if it comes between the subject and verb. This is not standard usage, but you may see it in novels.

As always, examples follow. (In these cases, *anyway* is functioning as a synonym for "at least.")

• Bob, anyway, didn't believe the silver-tongued preacher. (Bob, at least, didn't believe the silver-tongued preacher.)

**Spelling and Pronunciation**

This has nothing to do with commas, but the usage is so prevalent in some areas, I thought it worth the mention.

• *Anyway* does not have an *s* in the spelling. It is *anyway*, not *anyways*.

• You also need to be careful not to use it as two words when you mean one.

To ensure you're using the right version, replace the word *any* with *some* and see if it makes a difference. Suppose you broke down on the side of the road, and someone stopped to see what was wrong. You might say, "Is there *any way* you can help?" Using the replacement option mentioned above, you can see it works fine. "Is there *some way* you can help?"

As you see in the example below, though, it doesn't work with the one-word version—*anyway*. "I'm going to the mall *anyway*. When replaced by *some*, it doesn't work. "I'm going to the mall *some way*.

I hope this resolves your questions regarding commas with *anyway*. If it doesn't, feel free to send me an email.

# WHEN TO USE A COMMA BEFORE "DESPITE" OR "IN SPITE OF"

Before we start, we should discuss the differences between "despite" and "in spite of." The bottom line is there are no meaningful differences. They are as interchangeable as two words/phrases can be.

- He got promoted *despite* his bad track record.

- He got promoted *in spite of* his bad track record.

- She went to the party *despite* not wanting to go.

- She went to the party *in spite of* not wanting to go.

Whether to use one or the other comes down to choice. Some people say *despite* is slightly more formal, but it doesn't seem to make a difference. If you look at the Google Ngram below, it shows *despite* is far more popular than "in spite of." It doesn't show it here, but when I checked the English usage, it was about the same, and both showed a dramatic change beginning in the 1940–50 range.

Now that we've gotten the interchangeability question taken care of, let's look at comma usage. The question is whether a comma is necessary before—or after—either "despite" or "in spite of." The simple answer is no. A comma is not needed; however, there are those pesky exceptions. I'll cite the exceptions, but understand they are exceptions due to other reasons—ones we'll make mention of.

• If you use *despite* with a nonessential phrase, it requires a comma before the word and after the phrase. Keep in mind, though, that the requirement is due to the phrase being nonessential, not due to the appearance of *despite*.

Examples follow:

• He ordered the Chianti for dinner, despite it being a dry wine, and found he loved it.

• He ordered the Chianti for dinner, in spite of it being a dry wine, and found he loved it.

Take out the nonessential part, and you'll see.

• He ordered the Chianti for dinner and found he loved it.

Nonessential phrases are not needed grammatically, but the writer often wants them for stylistic purposes. Consider the following.

• Black snakes are common throughout North America, and, despite being harmless, people are afraid of them.

The sentence is fine from a grammar standpoint without the nonessential phrase, but it adds a lot with the phrase intact.

- Black snakes are common throughout North America, and people are afraid of them.

Then there are stylistic choices:

- The kids in the pool were getting sunburned despite having sunscreen on.

- The kids in the pool were getting sunburned, despite having sunscreen on.

In the examples above, the use of a comma is optional; in other words, it's a choice. Sometimes a writer may feel that adding the comma places more emphasis on the phrase that follows. Technically, the comma doesn't need to be there, but no one will complain if the writer puts it in.

# WHEN TO USE A COMMA WITH INSTEAD

Many people insert a comma before *instead* even though it is seldom necessary. Let's look at when a comma should and shouldn't be used. In most cases, a comma may *follow* the word but seldom precede it.

If *instead* is used as an adverb to introduce a sentence, it should be followed by a comma.

• The cost of tomatoes has risen dramatically. Instead, we should eat corn.

But if it is used at the end of a sentence, no comma is necessary.

• The cost of tomatoes has risen dramatically, so I think we'll eat corn instead.

Even if you turn it into a prepositional phrase, the comma is only required if that phrase introduces another clause.

• Instead of eating tomatoes, we'll eat corn.

If you turn it around, however, no comma is necessary.

- We'll eat corn instead of tomatoes.

I've seen a lot of writers use *instead* in the middle of the sentence, effectively turning the sentence into a comma splice.

- We planned on going to the opera to see *La Traviata*, instead, we went to the movies.

This is not an acceptable construction. If you wanted to express yourself in that way, you would need to use either a period or semicolon. And in both cases, *instead* would be followed by a comma.

- We planned on going to the opera to see *La Traviata*. Instead, we went to the movies.

- We planned on going to the opera to see *La Traviata*; instead, we went to the movies.

Either of the above examples is acceptable. It is simply a style choice.

# WHEN TO USE A COMMA BEFORE "IS" AND "WAS."

One of the more frequent mishaps I see with commas is in using them with *is* and *was*. With any luck, we'll get that squared away.

I'm going to tackle this one differently, though. Instead of trying to find rules or guidelines to explain why a comma should or should not be used, we're going to "wing it." And by "wing it," I mean use the "when you *hear* a pause, insert a comma" rule.

This is nothing accepted or recommended, but it usually works. At least, it works most of the time. Try it out with the examples below. The sentences are listed without the commas following *is*. Read the sentences aloud and place a comma when you hear a pause.

- The fact is since Rusty died, her connections have gotten stronger.

- If it is I'm sure we can arrange that.

- It is and it isn't, Ribs.

- Yeah, but the odd thing is he doesn't seem to be cooperating.

- As it is it's costing me extra.

- The problem is we can't prove anything.

- I tried my best to reason it out so we might blame Ortega, but the trouble is I believed him when he told us about the priest.

- The bottom line is if the Boswells come through, we get the dealers, and if they don't, we get the Boswells.

- The problem is all the witnesses are dead.

~

Now that you've done that, compare your answers to the following:

- The fact is **(comma needed)**, since Rusty died, her connections have gotten stronger.

- If it is **(comma needed)**, I'm sure we can arrange that.

- It is **(comma needed)**, and it isn't, Ribs.

- Yeah, but the odd thing is **(comma needed)**, he doesn't seem to be cooperating.

- As it is **(comma needed)**, it's costing me extra.

- The problem is **(comma needed)**, we can't prove anything.

- I tried my best to reason it out so we might blame Ortega, but the trouble is **(comma needed)**, I believed him when he told us about the priest.

- The bottom line is **(comma needed)**, if the Boswells come through, we get the dealers, and if they don't, we get the Boswells.

- The problem is **(comma needed)**, all the witnesses are dead.

# EVERYTHING YOU NEED TO KNOW ABOUT COMMAS

Now, let's analyze what we did. Strict grammarians may say some of our comma placement was wrong, but what matters is what you, the author, think. All the choices we made were style choices —meaning we could opt to either use or not use the commas. It depends on how you want it to sound and what you want to emphasize. Let's take a look at one of the sentences and use commas in different places.

---

The problem **is**, we can't prove anything.

The problem is we can't prove anything.

The **problem**, is we can't prove anything.

---

If read with pauses where the comma is and no pause where the comma isn't, each of the above sentences reads quite differently. The emphasis ends up being on the words in **bold.**

By the way, all our examples used *is*, but the same logic would have applied for *was*.

Now, on to the next chapter.

# LIKE AND SUCH AS, AND HOW TO USE THEM WITH COMMAS

*This* chapter will be slightly different. We'll be discussing how to use *like* and *such as* along with how to use commas with them.

*Like* and *such as* are often used interchangeably and for good reason—they are extremely close in meaning and usage.

I'll repeat this later, but *like* is often used in a comparative mode, while *such as* is more inclusive. Let's look at a few examples.

• Dogs such as Great Danes and poodles don't bite.

You don't use a comma before *such as* because it introduces a phrase that is a necessary part of the sentence. We can test this by removing the phrase to see if the sentence still means the same thing.

• Dogs don't bite.

We all know that's not true. Some dogs *do* bite; therefore, the phrase "such as Great Danes and poodles" is needed.

However, if you said, "Herding dogs, such as Australian shepherds and border collies, are very active," you would need commas.

Remove the phrase and see.

- Herding dogs are very active.

Not only does it make sense, it means the same thing. With the phrase intact, we're only adding information, and it's information that isn't needed.

When you use *like*, it tells us that what comes before it is to be used in a comparative manner to what comes after it. A few examples follow using both terms.

- She loves long-haired cats, such as the Persian and ragdoll.

- Her husband loves short-haired dogs, such as the boxer and Dalmatian.

- Her husband loves dogs like the German and Anatolian shepherds, but he can't tolerate the long hair.

Let's look at the sentences above. In the first one, we said, "She loves long-haired cats, such as the Persian and ragdoll." By using *such as*, we indicated that what followed was to be included as examples of long-haired cats; in other words, they *were* long-haired cats.

Example two was the same: Dalmatians and boxers are short-haired dogs.

However, in the third example, we said her husband loves dogs *like* the German and Anatolian shepherds, meaning he loves dogs that have something in common with them. Perhaps it is their size, traits, mannerisms, etc. However, he doesn't love the shepherds (they are long-haired dogs) but dogs like (similar to) them.

***Like* Is Used for Comparison**

We'll go through this again.

While *like* and *such as* are frequently interchangeable, there are differences. *Like* is used to compare what follows, and *such as* includes what follows. Sometimes it may seem like splitting hairs, but if you analyze the sentences below, you can see there is a difference.

- My grandson loves fruits like strawberries and cantaloupe.
- My grandson loves fruits, such as strawberries, blackberries, cantaloupe, and honeydew.

In the first example, we use *like* to say he loves fruits that are similar to strawberries and cantaloupe. It doesn't mean he likes those specific fruits; he may hate them but like fruits that are similar.

In the second example, we use *such as* to be specific—saying he loves strawberries, blackberries, cantaloupe, and honeydew.

👍 Remember to use *like* for comparisons and *such as* when you want to cite examples.

**Bottom Line**

I don't think anyone is going to misunderstand you if you use *like* instead of *such as* or vice versa, but it helps to know the difference.

Now that I've touted all this nonsense, let me say that *like* and *such as* are as interchangeable as any words I know. I've cited some differences that the strictest grammarians adhere to, but in everyday life, writers can, and should, use whichever word they want.

*Such as* comes across as more formal, and if that's the style you're aiming for, use it.

If you have a situation where it seems natural to use *such* as, then use it. If you think *like* sounds better, use it.

———————————————

# COMMAS BEFORE AND AFTER REGARDLESS

We've already discussed the complexity of when and where to use commas in your writing. In most cases, grammarians agree on the instances and even cite rigid rules they say should be applied. However, that's not the case with *regardless*.

Let's look at the rules recognized as rigid or at least semirigid. *Regardless* is similar to *anyway*, at least as far as comma use goes, so if you're comfortable with your understanding of how to use commas with *anyway*, then you'll probably be okay with how to use commas with *regardless*. If you still want to go over it, do so. If not, move to the next chapter.

When *regardless* functions as an adverb at the beginning of a sentence, you need a comma after it.

- Regardless, you're going to do as I say.

And it doesn't matter if it's a one-word introduction or multiple words.

- Regardless of the danger, we're going in there today.

Then we have the cases where *regardless* functions as part of a prepositional phrase and doesn't need a comma.

- She was terrified of vaccines regardless of the scientific evidence.

And no comma is necessary when *regardless* comes at the end of the sentence.

- He knew it was dangerous, but he decided to go regardless.

To sum it up:

- When *regardless* comes at the beginning of a sentence, you need a comma after it.
- When it is followed by an introductory phrase, the phrase is followed by a comma, not the word.
- If it comes at the end of a sentence, no comma is necessary.

There are times when a comma is not sufficient, and either a semicolon or period is needed.

✗ - He knew she didn't like dry wine, regardless, he ordered the Chianti.

✓ - He knew she didn't like dry wine; regardless, he ordered the Chianti.

✓ - He knew she didn't like dry wine. Regardless, he ordered the Chianti.

As you can see from the above examples, the comma was not the right choice. The sentence needed something stronger.

*Regardless* also forms a prepositional phrase, creating the well-known "regardless of."

We've already seen an example of a sentence beginning with such a phrase. We used it above. (Regardless of the danger, we're going in there today.)

Now we need to take a look at a prepositional phrase occurring midsentence.

- We prepared for the worst regardless of the optimistic reports.

- We prepared for the worst, regardless of the optimistic reports.

Most experts agree that the placement, or not, of a comma in this situation is a writer's choice. I usually decide based on how it sounds when I read it. If I pause when reading it, I use a comma. And if I don't pause, I leave the comma out.

# SO, AND WHEN TO USE A COMMA WITH IT

One of the more difficult things for me to learn regarding punctuation was when to use a comma with the word *so*.

The use of *so* didn't seem to fit with the normal instances of when to use commas with conjunctions. Sometimes it did, and other times it didn't. I looked it up in *Garner's Modern American Usage* book and CMOS (*The Chicago Manual of Style*).

As is often the case, those explanations left me more confused than when I started.

Finally, I stumbled on an explanation written on Grammarly's site. After reading the blog, I was able to grasp the subtleties of when—and when not to—use a comma with *so*.

I think one of the problems is that *so* is so versatile. It covers a lot of ground for such a little word. Let's look at how it's used.

1. *So* is used as *therefore*, to show the result or consequence of something.

2. *So* is used as *so that*, to show reason or purpose.

3. *So* is used to express *addition*, as in "and also." (Times have changed, and so has she.)

4. *So* is used as an intensifier, though it's often frowned upon when used that way.

5. *So* is used to agree or acknowledge the truth of something, as in "I heard it's so."

6. *So* is often used as a substitute for something already stated, as in "She didn't like his manners, and she told him *so*."

For right now, let's look at the first two examples.

**The Trick**

When you use *so*, substitute *therefore* or *so that* in your head. Say the sentence using those words. If *therefore* works, use a comma; if *so that* works better, do not use a comma. Make sure the sentence retains the same meaning.

One scenario that may mix you up is when you have the words *so that* written in a sentence. I've provided an example below.

- I couldn't care less about Grammarly's suggestion of a dangling modifier, *so that* advice was useless.

The presence of *so that* may throw you off at first, but if you carefully follow through with the substitution, you'll see it works. Try it with both options, but remember to substitute for *so* only, not for *so that*.

- I couldn't care less about Grammarly's suggestion of a dangling modifier *so that that* advice was useless.

- I couldn't care less about Grammarly's suggestion of a dangling modifier, *therefore* that advice was useless.

*Therefore* is the only substitution that works because you're only substituting for *so*, not for *so that*. In other words, if you substituted *so that*, the sentence would read as above: "I couldn't care less about Grammarly's suggestion of a dangling modifier, *so that that* advice was useless."

**More Examples**

• We stayed out all night, *so* we could see the meteor storm pass.

In some instances, the substitution doesn't seem to work. Look at the sentence above. I could substitute *so that* or *therefore* and have either one work.

But if you do the substitutions and then look closely at the sentences, there is a different meaning depending on which substitution you use.

• We stayed out all night, *therefore* we could see the meteor storm pass.

• We stayed out all night *so that* we could see the meteor storm pass.

In the first sentence, they stayed out all night, and as a *result*, they could see the meteor storm.

In the second sentence, the *reason* they stayed out all night was so they could see the meteor storm.

Two more examples follow.

• We built a fire *so* we kept warm.

• We built a fire, *so* we kept warm.

If you analyze the sentences, you'll see they are similar to those above. In the first sentence, they built a fire *in order* to keep warm (reason or purpose). In the second, they built a fire, and as a *result*, they kept warm.

Substituting *therefore* or *so that* doesn't clarify things enough in the above cases because either one of the substitutions will work. You have to know what message is being conveyed. Are you trying to give the *reason* they built the fire? Or are you relating the *result*?

**Bottom Line** (for this part)

The bottom line is simple. If the sentence works with both substitutions, use a comma with the one that reflects result (*therefore*) and no comma with the one that reflects reason (*so that*).

**Other Uses of *So***

When *so* is used as an adverb meaning "to a great extent" or "to a degree," as in "I love you *so* much" or "That felt *so* good," there is no need for a comma before or immediately following it.

Once exception I can think of is if you said something similar to "I love you so, but I can't marry you."

In that case, you are adding an independent clause after *so*, and it's that clause that requires the comma (preceding *but*).

When *so* is used as a substitute for something already stated, as in "She didn't like his manners, and she told him *so*," no comma is necessary preceding or following *so* (assuming words follow it and no other construction demands a comma). Usually, when used in this manner, *so* comes at the end of a sentence: "Have you finished packing?" "I think *so*."

When *so* is used to mean "in the same way," no comma is needed, as in "She swam like a fish, and *so* did he."

When used to indicate a measurement (usually accompanied by a gesture), as in "That fish was *so* long" or meaning "to an extent," as in "A man can only do *so* much." In either case, no commas are necessary before or after.

When *so* is used as an introductory word (beginning a sentence), as in "So you finally got here" or "So you arrived," no commas are needed; in fact, in most cases, *so* isn't needed. Look at the sentences without *so*. "You finally got here" and "You arrived." Both are fine without *so*.

There are other ways to use *so*, but I can't think of any that would require using a comma immediately preceding or following it.

————————————

# THAT IS, NAMELY, AND FOR EXAMPLE

*That is, namely,* and *for example* are three expressions that are usually followed by commas; however, there are recommended ways of treating them that differ from the typical practice.

*The Chicago Manual of Style* has the following to say:

Expressions of the type "that is" are traditionally followed by a comma. They are best preceded by an em dash or a semicolon rather than a comma, or the entire phrase they introduce may be enclosed in parentheses or em dashes.

**CMOS**

Let's look at a few examples:

- There are dogs that are far worse biters than pit bulls—*namely,* rat terriers and other small dogs.

- The water district (*that is,* John Moore) voted to increase rates again.

- The water district raised rates again; *that is*, the head of the committee raised them to get his wife a new car.

- Our cat's room held proof of her hunting prowess—*for example*, rat and squirrel tails, remnants of frogs and lizards, and feathers from various birds.

In this same section, CMOS goes on to say:

When *or* is used in a sense analogous to "that is" (to mean "in other words"), the phrase it introduces is usually set off by commas.

**CMOS**

- The surveyor's tool, *or* transit, is used to align points, determine levels, and measure distances.

When *or* is used this way (as "in other words"), it places the phrase it introduces as nonessential, therefore necessitating commas on either side of the phrase. As you can see in the example, *transit* is merely additional information and not necessary to the sentence.

———————————————

# WHEN TO USE A COMMA BEFORE THOUGH

There is a fairly good guideline to follow on this rule. You should use a comma before *though*, when *though* could be replaced with *however*, but not when it represents "despite the fact."

• My grandson loves swimming. My granddaughter loves skating, though. (however)

• My grandson walked home from school though it was raining. (despite the fact)

*Although* and *even though* can be lumped in with *though* as far as comma use goes; in fact, they are almost interchangeable. *Although* is interchangeable with the exception that it is looked upon as being more formal. *Even though* is almost the same, but it expresses a more emphatic sense.

*Even though* is also used frequently to introduce nonessential clauses. Examples follow.

- "Bob wears a mask all the time, even though he's not sick." Or

  - "Bob wears a mask all the time, even when he's not sick."

That's it for *though*. Simple, wasn't it? Not all rules with commas are so easy, though I wish they could be.

# WHEN TO USE A COMMA BEFORE TOO

If you grew up in the last sixty years or so, you may have been instructed to place a comma before the word *too*, especially if it carried the meaning of "also" or "in addition to."

This instruction often included a command to do so whether *too* occurred midsentence or at the end of the sentence. Now it's time to revisit that antiquated bit of advice and see if it holds water.

In most cases, you don't need commas with *too* (or also), and that's true whether it is midsentence or at the end.

- He likes wine, spirits, and brandy too.

- She too likes blond men.

In the first and second examples, *too* is used as a synonym for *also*. Despite that, it gets no comma.

One time when *too* requires a comma is when it separates the verb from its object.

Let's assume that a person was mugged on a city street. A witness came forward and said, "I saw him do it. I saw him."

Then you stepped forward and said, "I saw, too, that he did it."

This wouldn't be the most common way to see the phrase written, but it's easy to imagine it happening in dialogue in a novel.

Although commas aren't necessary in the first examples, commas with *too*, like many other words, are the option of the author. If an author wants to emphasize a change of pace or thought, they should use a comma. When a person is reading, there is a big difference between "I, too, like reading," and "I too like reading."

It's the same as we mentioned before. Using the comma to create a pause in the flow of reading. This kind of choice is part of what makes up the writer's voice. Along with many other factors, it's what identifies that writer and makes him or her unique.

Read the following sentences aloud, and make sure you *don't* pause where the commas aren't and *do* pause where they are. You'll notice the difference.

- She likes red wine. I however prefer white.

- She likes red wine. I, however, prefer white.

The bottom line is simple. *The Chicago Manual of Style* takes a stance on this, and they say it is unnecessary to use a comma before *too* at the end of a sentence. They also say that unless the writer wants an abrupt change, commas are unnecessary midsentence.

As is often the case, the decision is up to the writer. Do it as you see fit but be consistent.

# POSSIBLE UNNECESSARY COMMA AFTER AN ESSENTIAL WHICH, WHERE, OR WHO CLAUSE

When you're trying to determine whether to use a comma before *which*, *where*, or *who*, you need to determine the function of the clause that follows the word. If what follows these words is essential to the sentence, you don't use a comma, but when what follows is not essential, put a comma before the word.

I tried to keep my explanation simple, but let's break it down with examples.

- I want to go to a country where they have very low taxes.

In that instance, you don't use a comma because the clause "where they have very low taxes" is essential to the meaning of the sentence. Now consider this sentence:

- My granddaughter, who loves math and science, is very intelligent.

To test it, take out the clause and see if it works. You'd be left with the following:

- I want to go to a country.

- My granddaughter is very intelligent.

As you can see, the phrase was needed in the first sentence but not in the second.

**When Should We Place a Comma before a Relative Clause?**

Here are some examples of sentences with both essential and nonessential clauses.

- Are you the guy who won the poker tournament?

- I want to watch a movie that has good acting.

- I need to move to a city where the crime rate and cost of living are low.

- His tournament winnings, which broke all records, were the result of one huge pot.

- Two people mentioned Austin, where he eventually found peace, as the place to settle down.

- Johnny Depp, who is the best actor I know, won the Oscar for best actor.

Now, remove the clauses and look at the sentences.

- Are you the guy?

- I want to watch a movie.

- I need to move to a city.

- His tournament winnings were the result of one huge pot.

- Two people mentioned Austin as the place to settle down.

- Johnny Depp won the Oscar for best actor.

As you can see, the first three sentences don't mean the same thing they do with the clause attached, while the next three could stand on their own.

Some sentences may appear to contain nonessential clauses, but when closely analyzed, what seems to be the nonessential part is, in fact, necessary. Below is an example.

- People who are addicted to caffeine don't mind drinking a cup or two of coffee before going to bed.

If you test for nonessential phrases (removing the phrase), you'll see the sentence needs that phrase. Take a look.

If you remove "who are addicted to caffeine," it leaves us a complete sentence and one that makes sense, but it doesn't convey the same meaning as the original.

- People don't mind drinking a cup or two of coffee before going to bed.

As mentioned, while that is a complete sentence, the meaning it conveys isn't the same. Now it's saying all people are okay with drinking a cup or two of coffee before going to bed, and that's simply not right.

We need to know it's those who are addicted to caffeine who don't mind drinking a cup or two. The information isn't necessary for forming a sentence, but it is critical for conveying your thoughts properly.

**Summary**

Many people, even writers, ignore the importance of commas, but commas have a major impact on whatever is written. As you read the following sentences, pause at the commas and do not pause where there are none.

- "Immigrants who commit crimes should be punished."

- "Immigrants, who commit crimes, should be punished."

- "It's time to eat, Mollie."

- "It's time to eat Mollie."

Carefully read the two sentences above; you'll notice a big difference. In the first, we're saying the immigrants who commit crimes should be punished. That may refer to one-tenth of one percent of them, or it may refer to 50 percent. The point is, we're talking about only those immigrants who commit crimes.

In the second sentence, we're saying *all* immigrants commit crimes and should be punished. That's a big difference, a *really* big difference.

In the third sentence, we can picture someone calling their dog (named Mollie) to eat dinner.

In the last sentence (read it without pausing), we can imagine poor Mollie, roasted and placed on a silver platter in the center of the kitchen table.

Although many nonessential phrases are introduced with relative pronouns, such as *who, which, where,* etc., you also need to look out for nonessential phrases that *don't* begin with a relative pronoun. Look at the following example.

- Kate Winslet, who was the actress from *The Titanic,* is a very talented person.

- Kate Winslet, the actress from *The Titanic,* is a very talented person.

If we remove the nonessential part of the sentences, we're left with the same thing.

- "Kate Winslet is a very talented person."

A close look at the lessons regarding commas reveals many of the comma issues associated with nonessential clauses. When faced with whether to use a comma, look at that first, then decide if you need one.

# WHEN TO USE AND NOT USE COMMAS

There are a few hard-and-fast rules and one I see broken frequently. I'm guilty of it myself. Which rule?

Do *not* use commas after *such as*, *like*, and *although*—unless what follows is a nonessential clause (unnecessary).

I know we've covered *like* and *such as*, but this is slightly different.

Examples follow:

✘ I love Italian foods such as, ravioli, lasagna, and gnocchi.

✓ I love Italian foods, such as ravioli, lasagna, and gnocchi.

✓ I love Italian foods, such as ravioli, lasagna, and gnocchi, but not dishes that include seafood.

Commas are required when the clause is not needed for the sentence to be true. Take the clause out and see: "I love Italian foods but not dishes that include seafood."

The next few examples deal with using commas with the words *although* and *like*.

✗ I like Italian food although, I eat steaks every week (no comma after *although*).

✓ I like Italian food, although I eat steaks every week.

✗ Even though I love Italian food, I eat things like, burgers and hot dogs (no comma after *like*).

✓ Even though I love Italian food, I eat things like burgers and hot dogs.

**Do not use commas** in front of dependent words, like *because, when, if, until,* and *unless*. (For a more complete list of dependent words, see the list on my website.)

✗ The dog was panting, because it had just chased the mailman.

✓ The dog was panting because it had just chased the mailman.

✗ We'll go to the mall, when your mother gets home.

✓ We'll go to the mall when your mother gets home.

**When to Use a Comma**

**Use a comma** after a dependent clause that starts a sentence.

- "When I went to the bank, I made a deposit."

As mentioned, a dependent clause cannot stand on its own. It is not a complete sentence, and that's why it's called a dependent clause; it needs the rest of the sentence to support it.

Commas always follow these clauses when they're found at the start of a sentence, but when a dependent clause ends the sentence, it no longer requires a comma.

- "When I went to the bank, I made a deposit"

- "I made a deposit when I went to the bank."

**Use commas** to separate independent clauses when they are joined by any of these seven coordinating conjunctions: *and, but, for, or, nor, so, yet.*

✅ "I went to the bank *and* made a deposit." (No comma before *and* because "made a deposit" is not a complete sentence.)

✅ I went to the bank, *and* I made a deposit. A comma is necessary because "I made a deposit" is a complete sentence.

❌ I went to the bank, *and* made a deposit. (No comma is necessary.)

❌ I went to the bank *and* I made a deposit. (Comma is necessary after *bank*.)

And don't forget that the comma goes before the conjunction (*and, but, for, or, nor, so, yet*), not after it.

There is a case where a comma also goes after the connecting word. Look at the following, which you'll see later as well.

• A semicolon should not be used in place of a colon. It's not a good substitute, and, despite its name association, it doesn't want to be a colon.

Notice the comma after *and*. We need a comma there because the phrase that follows—despite its name association—is a nonessential clause; it's not needed. Take it out and see.

• A semicolon should not be used in place of a colon. It's not a good substitute, and it doesn't want to be a colon.

As you can see, we still need the comma preceding *and* because it joins two independent clauses.

**Dependent markers** are words added to the beginning of an independent clause that make it a dependent clause. The following is a list of those words:

- after
- although
- as
- as if
- because
- before
- even if
- even though
- if
- in order to
- since
- though
- unless
- until
- whatever
- when
- whenever
- whether
- while

An example might be:

- I made a deposit *when* I went to the bank.

Notice that "I made a deposit" and "I went to the bank" are both independent clauses, but by adding *when* to the beginning of the second clause, it becomes a dependent clause because you didn't just make a deposit, you made it *when* you went to the bank.

Another example could be shown by turning the sentence around.

- When I went to the bank, I made a deposit.

Note that we need a comma after *bank* in this situation because it falls under the rule mentioned earlier: use a comma after a dependent clause that starts a sentence.

Now we're about to get confusing, so put on your learner's hat.

**Independent Marker Word**

An independent marker word is a connecting word used at the beginning of an independent clause. These words can always begin a complete sentence.

When the second independent clause in a sentence has an independent marker word, a semicolon is needed before the independent marker word (yes, that dreaded semicolon). These words are also called "conjunctive adverbs."

☑ I wasn't planning on going to the bank; *however*, I needed to make a deposit.

As you can see, *however* joins the two independent clauses with a semicolon.

☑ I don't want to go to the bank; *nevertheless*, I need to make a deposit.

☑ "I'll be driving down Fourth Street; *therefore*, I'll stop by the bank and make a deposit.

**A Partial List of Independent Marker Words/Conjunctive Adverbs**

- also

- consequently
- fortunately
- furthermore
- hopefully
- however
- in addition
- in fact
- instead
- likewise
- meanwhile
- moreover
- nevertheless
- on the other hand
- otherwise
- therefore
- unfortunately

Other words could be added to this list, but these are the more commonly used ones.

**Use commas** before every sequence of three numbers when writing a number larger than 999. (Two exceptions are when writing years and house numbers.)

For example, you would write numbers this way: 4,176 or 10,000 or 1,304,687.

But you would write, "He was born in 1972" and "She lives at 2419 Canal Street."

~

Use commas before and after nonessential words, phrases, and clauses—that is, parts of the sentence that interrupt it without changing the essential meaning.

Below is an example of such a sentence. It's a sentence I used previously, but it's a good example.

☑ A semicolon should not be used in place of a colon. It's not a good substitute, and, despite its name association, it doesn't want to be a colon.

Note that this breaks the rule that says not to place a comma after a coordinating conjunction, but an analysis will show that the comma after *substitute* is required because it separates two independent clauses, and the comma after *and* is required because it precedes a nonessential phrase ("despite its name association"). That phrase is nonessential because if you remove it, the sentence still makes sense and the meaning doesn't change.

☑ A semicolon should not be used in place of a colon. It's not a good substitute, and it doesn't want to be a colon.

With the preceding sentence, you can eliminate that comma by rewording the sentence to make the second clause dependent:

☑ A semicolon should not be used in place of a colon. It's not a good substitute and doesn't want to be a colon.

Below are a few examples of combining appositives with nonessential phrases.

☑ My wife, Mikki, who loves to shop, is at the fabric store.

☑ My brother Chris, who loves to drink, is at the store getting beer.

In the first example, we used commas to offset *Mikki,* as it is nonessential. Since I only have one wife, naming Mikki is unnecessary. We also offset the nonessential phrase "who loves to shop," as it is not necessary. As you can see below, the sentence works fine without either of these nonessential phrases.

☑ My wife is at the fabric store.

In the second example, we don't offset *Chris* with commas as I have more than one brother, so including his name is necessary. The nonessential phrase follows the same reasoning as the first example. Now, look at the essential parts of that sentence.

☑ My brother Chris is at the store getting beer.

There is a time (when using a nonessential clause) you should opt for a different punctuation mark. I cover this later on in the chapter dealing with dashes, but it won't hurt to touch on it here.

We've gone over nonessential phrases and how you should use commas to offset them, but there is an exception. (Isn't there always?)

If that additional bit of information contains commas of its own, use an em dash on either side of it instead of a comma; it makes it easier to understand. I've included an example below, where the sentence is presented both ways—with and without the em dash.

• My van, the one with the wheelchair ramp, automatic doors, and winch, is black.

• My van—the one with the wheelchair ramp, automatic doors, and winch—is black.

As you can see, the use of the em dashes makes the sentence easier to read than the one without em dashes.

**Use commas** to separate items in a series of three or more:

- My brother Chris picked up hot dogs, hamburgers, potato chips, and Coke when he went to the store.

If he had only picked up two items, the commas would not have been necessary.

- My brother Chris picked up hot dogs and hamburgers when he went to the store.

And notice in the first example, there is no comma following *Coke* or before *went*. You only use commas to separate the items in the list.

**Use a comma** after introductory adverbs.

☑ Finally, he got home with the food.

☑ At last, I could breathe.

Also insert a comma when phrases like "on the other hand," *however*, and *furthermore* start a sentence.

No comma is necessary with *however* when it is used to mean "no matter how" or "to whatever extent."

- *However* you do it, get it done.

- *However* it has to be done, just do it.

Look at the sentences with those meanings substituted.

- No matter how you do it, get it done.

- Whatever has to be done, just do it.

**Use a comma** when attributing quotes.

The rule for where the comma goes depends on where the attribution is placed within the sentence.

If the attribution comes before the quote, place the comma prior to and outside the quotations marks.

- My brother said, "I picked up some beer."

But if the attribution comes after the quote, put the comma inside the closing quotation marks.

- "I got some beer," said my brother (or "my brother said").

**Use a comma** to separate each element in an address. Also use a comma after a city-state combination within a sentence.

✅ I work downtown at 1212 Milam Street, Houston, Texas 77070.

or

✅ I love to visit San Francisco, California, one of my favorite cities.

**Use commas** to separate full dates (weekday, month and day, and year). Separate the parts of an address from each other as well as from the rest of the sentence.

✅ August 1, 1960, was the day I was born.

Keep the commas even if you add the name of a day.

✅ Friday, April 21, 2015, is a day I'll not soon forget.

**You don't need to add a comma** when the sentence contains only the month and year.

✅ February 2015 was a disastrous month.

✅ The meeting is set for October 2029 in Philadelphia.

I learned this because in many of my books, I'll list the date and location at the heading of each chapter. I used to use commas to separate month from year until my editor corrected me.

**Use a comma** when the first word of the sentence is a freestanding yes or no. In other words, you could have stopped with the one-word answer.

☑ I asked my brother if he got chips, and he said, "Yes, I got chips as well as pretzels."

He could have simply said yes, but he added more.

**Use a comma** when directly addressing someone or something in a sentence.

☑ Tommy asked, "Can I go out to play, Mom?"

**Use a comma** to offset negation in a sentence.

☑ "I made a deposit, not a withdrawal, when I stopped at the bank."

Notice that this is similar to the use of commas with nonessential clauses. If you remove the negative part of the sentence, the meaning of the primary sentence stays the same.

- "I made a deposit when I stopped at the bank."

There are plenty of rules regarding commas, but most of the common are mentioned here. Those that aren't—like where and when to place commas between adjectives when they are used as descriptors—are easy enough to find.

———————

# WHEN TO USE A COMMA BEFORE EVEN

## When to Use a Comma before *Even*

*Even*, when used as a verb, is usually not the issue when considering whether to use a comma.

- The boss told him to even out the concrete. (verb form)

It's when *even* is combined with other words that you need to be on alert. A few of those words/phrases are: "even so", "even if," "even though," etc. The confusion occurs when *even* functions as an adjective or adverb.

- Their vacation in Italy went well, but even so, they were eager to get home.

- I know you didn't like Naples, but we should go there one more time even so.

You normally don't need a comma with *even*, but there are a few scenarios where a comma might be necessary. One such case is when *even* is used as an adverb and comes at the end of the sentence or is used as an introductory word or phrase.

- *Even* his mother knew he was guilty.
- *Even now*, after getting COVID, he refuses to wear a mask.
- The punishment was harsh—cruel, *even*.

There are other cases where *even* might occur in the middle of a sentence and require commas, but in those cases, it is usually due to it being a part of a nonessential phrase.

- The 1950s was a banner decade for blacks entering the major leagues, but *even then*, the discrimination continued.

Note that if grammar is taken to the extreme, a comma after *but* is required to set off the nonessential phrase "even then." But when the nonessential phrase is short, as this one is, the additional comma is typically omitted.

To sum it up, regardless of whether it's "even if," "even so," "even though," "even when," or any other *even*, a comma is necessary to offset a nonessential clause. If the clause is needed, *do not* use a comma.

Now, let's move on to *if* and see if we can figure out when to use a comma with it.

# WHEN TO USE A COMMA WITH "IF"

Much of the time, the decision to use a comma with *if* comes down to a style preference, and it will usually be a decision regarding whether to add emphasis to the sentence. Consider the two sentences below.

- I asked him to help me pour the concrete if he could.

- I asked him to help me pour the concrete, if he could.

In the first sentence, it's a plain and simple request, but the second one comes across a little differently. Say each one, placing a pause where the comma is, and you'll see what I mean.

∽

ANOTHER AREA where commas come into play is when *if* is followed by an introductory phrase. This occurs with many words, not just *if*. Some of the common ones are *although, as, because, since, when, while*.

. . .

- *BECAUSE* SHE GOT A TATTOO, she was grounded.

- *If* you aren't home by midnight, forget about going to the beach.

- *While* you're brooding in your room, remember what brought that about.

- *When* you think about what you did wrong, you'll understand why I punished you.

- *As* I was saying, no more dates until I say so.

ALL THE ABOVE HAVE THE same thing in common. They introduce a subordinate clause—that is, a clause that doesn't stand on its own. The reverse, however, is not true. Take a few of the sentences above and turn them around. You'll see what I mean. The comma isn't necessary.

- YOU'LL UNDERSTAND why I punished you *when* you think about what you did wrong.

- She was grounded *because* she got a tattoo.

- Forget about going to the beach *if* you aren't home by midnight.

SINCE WE WERE DISCUSSING introductory phrases, we should look at a few. So for those of you who enjoy grammatical terms, here you go.

INTRODUCTORY PHRASES that should be followed by a comma include absolute, infinitive, nonessential, participial, and prepositional phrases of more than four words.

In case you're not a grammar nut, let's look at each of these phrases in a more simplistic manner.

**Absolute Phrases**

Absolute phrases modify sentences. They are usually set off by commas, mostly because they are typically nonessential. An example of one at the end of a sentence follows.

- He fought in the war as a Marine, his body riddled with shrapnel.

The above is an absolute phrase, but so is the sentence below.

- His stitches closed and wounds healed, he decided to go back to war.

**Infinitive Phrases**

Infinitive phrases might present themselves as adjectives, adverbs, or nouns. Below are examples of each.

- *To visit Italy* is my biggest dream.

Here, "to visit Italy" is functioning as the subject.

- On our trip to Italy, my wife brought plenty of books *to read*.

The infinitive "to read" functions as an adjective, and "on our trip to Italy" functions as a prepositional phrase.

In the following sentence, we'll once again look at a prepositional phrase, but it will also have an infinitive phrase functioning as an adverb.

*After the helicopter crash*, he risked almost certain death "to search" for his fellow soldiers.

"After the helicopter crash" served as the prepositional phrase, and "to search" functioned as the infinitive operating as an adverb.

Here are infinitive phrases functioning as direct objects.

HE BLEW on the dice *to increase* his luck.

You were told *to leave* at once.

**Participial Phrase**

The last phrase we'll cover is the participial phrase. A participle may be followed by an adverb, a prepositional phrase, an adverb clause, or any combination of these. A few examples follow.

*Singing in front of thousands of people*, the performer kept her composure and delivered a stellar rendition.

*Tiptoeing through the jungle*, the soldier barely kept his cool.

*Stunned by the percussion grenade*, the soldier sought a place to hide.

As usual, the introductory phrase is followed by a comma, but participial phrases are preceded by commas even when they complete the sentence.

After dealing, the poker players calculated the odds, then bet, *shutting out all distractions*.

# WHEN TO USE A COMMA BEFORE "UNLESS" AND "UNTIL"

*Unless* can only be used at the start of a dependent clause, and this means you will almost never need a comma before *unless*.

You shouldn't go to the prom unless you have a date.

He refused to go on the mission unless he had an extra gun.

Under the right circumstances and phrased differently, the clause introduced by *unless* could have been an independent clause, but as it is, they don't mean the same thing without the other clause.

There aren't many instances I can think of where you'd need a comma preceding *unless*, but there are a few. One of them is if you introduced a nonessential clause with the word. An example follows.

Most professional gamblers find it comforting that, *unless they have a run of bad luck*, Texas Hold 'Em will send them home with full wallets.

# USING A COMMA BEFORE SUBORDINATE CLAUSES

*I*n a perfect world, you'd recognize a subordinate clause when you saw one.

A subordinate clause—or dependent clause—begins with a subordinate conjunction or relative pronoun. Like all clauses, it has both a subject and verb, but the clause does not form a complete sentence. Below are a few examples of each.

• After he went to the bank, he blew the money he withdrew while gambling at the racetrack.

• As soon as she gets here, we're leaving.

• That is the book I want to buy.

• Whatever you want, I'll get you.

• Whose bike is that anyway?

**BELOW IS a list of subordinate conjunctions.**

## Subordinate conjunction list

| AFTER | ALTHOUGH | AS | AS IF |
|---|---|---|---|
| as long as | as much as | As soon as | as though |
| because | before | Even | even if |
| even though | if | if only | if when |
| If then | inasmuch | in order that | Just as |
| lest | now | Now that | once |
| provided | Provided that | Rather than | since |
| so that | supposing | than | that |
| though | till | unless | until |
| when | whenever | where | whereas |
| wherever | whether | which | While |
| who | whoever | Why | |

**Here are the relative pronouns:**

## List of Relative pronouns:

| That | What | Whatever |
|---|---|---|
| Whatsoever | When | Whenever |
| Where | Wheresoever | Wherever |
| Which | Whichever | Whichsoever |
| Who | Whoever | Whom |
| Whomever | Whomsoever | Whose |
| Whosever | Whosoever | Why |

Please note that many of these are seldom used in writing and even less in normal conversation.

Just remember, the commas come *after* the subordinate conjunction when it is at the beginning of the sentence. Subordinate Clause + Comma + Main Clause.

But when the subordinate clause follows the primary clause, no comma precedes it (usually). Main Clause + No comma + Subordinate Clause.

I said *usually* in the paragraph above because if the clause that follows the primary clause is nonessential (as we've mentioned), it takes a comma before it.

The bottom line is easy. Although there are "rules" that govern when to place commas in most instances, the final decision is up to the author, and that decision should be made for the sake of clarity.

# USING A COMMA WHEN YOU HEAR A PAUSE

*I*n a way, this is a continuation of what we began with "When to Use a Comma with *Is* and *Was*." It does, however, expand the examples beyond the word *is*.

WHEN YOU HEAR A PAUSE, this implies that everyone is reading the words on a page either aloud or in their head. I can't swear to that, but I believe it holds true for most, so let's presume it does and continue as if it were so. To start with, I'll use a silly explanation, but it's one that drives the point home.

MY WIFE and I had an animal sanctuary for more than twenty-five years. One of our dogs was a big, burly boxer named Mollie.

Every night, when it was time for dinner, my wife would call the animals, and when she got to Mollie, she'd say, "Time to eat, Mollie."

So, when she *said* it, it sounded as if she had used a comma, but one time, she left written instructions for the dog watchers because we were going to be out of town for the weekend. On the page for how to feed the dogs (yes, there were pages of instructions), she wrote:

When it's time for dinner, make sure to go to the door and call loudly,

"Time to eat Mollie."

"And that's it?" the dog watcher asked.

"And you better be hungry," I said, "because Mollie's a big girl. Surely enough for a half dozen people. Even with that, you'll have leftovers."

I suffered through a few glares from my wife, and those were followed by miles of silence as we drove to the airport.

**Comma Splices and Stylistic Choices**

One occasion when many writers opt to do things differently is when short clauses are involved. Some writers prefer to use a comma instead of a period or semicolon. Examples follow.

• Small dogs don't bite, they bark.

• Use commas, don't be a psycho.

Long ago, when Strunk and White, authors of *The Elements of Style*, administered advice to so many, they railed against examples like this.

This is no longer the case. Even the venerable *Chicago Manual of Style* has acknowledged that writers have CMOS's support for style decisions such as the above.

# EVERYTHING YOU NEED TO KNOW ABOUT COMMAS

~

IN THE SENTENCES ABOVE, the commas should technically be periods or semicolons, but if a writer feels a sentence sounds better with a comma, so be it.

However, there is a problem with this method as a guideline, and that is, if you *hear* the pause and think a comma is needed, it may be a semicolon, or a colon, or a period that's needed instead. If it's a short sentence, you should be all right, but if not, you may end up with a comma splice (run-on sentence).

This guideline goes a long way in supporting the idea that if you aren't sure of the rule regarding where to place a comma, use your voice. Speak the sentence out loud, and place a comma where you *hear* a pause.

This isn't ideal, and it isn't failsafe, but it's better than guessing.

ANOTHER TIME when a comma is often optional is when using "not only . . . but also." In most cases, it isn't necessary, such as in the first example below.

☑ "She was not only beautiful but intelligent."

If an author wanted to add emphasis, though, they could put a comma after *beautiful*, as in the second example.

☑ "She was not only beautiful, but intelligent."

You'll notice in both examples, that *also* was not used, only *but*. This is a writer's choice as well. Many writers leave *also* out, letting readers assume it as a given.

. . .

THERE ARE other times when this method can help. There are comma "rules" that sometimes need to be broken for clarification.

In the following sentence, there should be no comma (technically) because the *and* does not join two independent clauses.

- I saw the boss was busy and prepared to leave.

When you read that sentence, it isn't clear who is prepared to leave. Was it the boss or you?

However, with a comma inserted, it clears things up. It lets the reader know it was *you*, not the boss, who was prepared to leave.

- I saw the boss was busy, and prepared to leave.

Here's another one where the comma changes not only the grammar but the meaning of the sentence.

- Ever since Ancient Rome, soldiers have worn shoes (which/that) protected their feet.

- Ever since Ancient Rome, soldiers have worn shoes, which protected their feet.

IN THE FIRST EXAMPLE, without the comma following *shoes*, you're saying that ever since Ancient Rome, soldiers have worn shoes that protected their feet—as opposed to shoes that didn't. So maybe they wore sandals that offered no protection for the tops of their feet.

In the second example, with the comma following *shoes*, you're saying that ever since Ancient Rome, soldiers have worn shoes (which, by the way, protected their feet). In other words, prior to that time, they didn't wear shoes.

Depending on comma usage, there is a big difference in meaning.

Let's look at one more.

- The welders who never missed a day of work were given a week of vacation at Christmas.

- The welders, who never missed a day of work, were given a week of vacation at Christmas.

In the first example, we're saying the welders who didn't miss work got the vacation.

In the second, we're saying the welders (who, by the way, didn't miss work) got the vacation.

So in one case, all the welders got a vacation, and in the other, only the welders who didn't miss work got it.

The bottom line is simple. I don't expect the majority of you to learn all the rules of when and where to place commas in your writing. For those of you who try and get most of them right—great. For the others, practice the pause method. It will help you get the majority of your commas placed correctly.

One final note. Many people (writers included) use semicolons as if they were acceptable in place of commas. They're not. Semicolons need to be used only when and where they are called for. You can read about how to use them in any good book on grammar or punctuation. I have two you can refer to: *Simply Put: The Plain English Grammar Guide* and *Punctuation: The Ultimate Guide*.

# ACKNOWLEDGMENTS

Many thanks to all those who helped during the pre-editing phase of the book. And special thanks to JJ Toner for his many suggestions.

In addition, it is with great honor that I give eternal gratitude to my wife and all four of my grandkids. They give me the inspiration to keep going.

# ABOUT THE AUTHOR

Giacomo Giammatteo is the author of gritty crime dramas about murder, mystery, and family. He also writes nonfiction books, including the No Mistakes Careers, No Mistakes Publishing, No Mistakes Grammar, and No Mistakes Writing series.

When Giacomo isn't writing, he's helping his wife take care of the animals in their sanctuary. At last count, they had forty-five—eleven dogs, one horse, six cats, and twenty-six pigs.

Oh, and one crazy—and very large—wild boar, who takes walks with Giacomo every day and also happens to be his best buddy.

[ Image: unknown.png ]
nomistakespublishing.com
gg@giacomog.com

ALSO BY GIACOMO GIAMMATTEO

YOU CAN SEE ALL MY BOOKS HERE.

*And you can buy them on the platform of your choice.*

This brings up a thought: With more than eighty books out now, it is becoming difficult to try to update the list at the back of all of them. If you want to know what books I have out, use the link above, which takes you to my website, or download the latest copy of my GG recommended reading list, which is free.

**Nonfiction**

**Careers**

*No Mistakes Resumes, Book I of No Mistakes Careers*

*No Mistakes Interviews, Book II of No Mistakes Careers*

**Grammar**

*Misused Words, No Mistakes Grammar, Volume I*

*Misused Words for Business, No Mistakes Grammar, Volume II*

*More Misused Words, No Mistakes Grammar, Volume III*

*Visual Grammar* (This is a compilation of volumes I–III with a bit of new information added. It also includes pictures and is the world's first visual grammar book)

*Misused Words and Then Some, No Mistakes Grammar, Volume V*

*Simply Put: The Plain English Grammar Guide*

*How to Capitalize Anything*

**More Grammar**

*No Mistakes Grammar Bites, Volume I: Lie, Lay, Laid, and It's and Its*

*No Mistakes Grammar Bites, Volume II: Good and Well, and Then and Than*

*No Mistakes Grammar Bites, Volume III: That, Which, and Who, and There Is and There Are*

*No Mistakes Grammar Bites, Volume IV: Affect and Effect, and Accept and Except*

*No Mistakes Grammar Bites, Volume V: You're and Your, and They're, There, and Their*

*No Mistakes Grammar Bites, Volume VI: Passed and Past, and Into, In to and In*

*No Mistakes Grammar Bites, Volume VII: Farther and Further, and Onto, On, and On To*

*No Mistakes Grammar Bites, Volume VIII: Anxious and Eager, and Different From and Different Than*

*No Mistakes Grammar Bites, Volume IX, A While and Awhile, and Envy and Jealousy*

*No Mistakes Grammar Bites, Volume X, Could've and Should've, and Irony and Coincidence*

*No Mistakes Grammar Bites, Volume XI: "Quotation Marks and How to Punctuate Them" and "Plurals of Compound Nouns"*

*No Mistakes Grammar Bites, Volume XII: "Latin Abbreviations"*

*No Mistakes Grammar Bites, Volume XIII: "Redundancies" and "Ax to Grind"*

*No Mistakes Grammar Bites Volume XIV: "Superlatives and How We Use them Wrong"*

*No Mistakes Grammar Bites Volume XV: "Shoo-in and Shoe-in" and "Horse Racing Sayings"*

*No Mistakes Grammar Bites Volume XVI: "Which and What" and "Since and Because"*

*No Mistakes Grammar Bites Volume XVII: "Hyphens, and When to Use Them" and "Em Dashes and En Dashes"*

*No Mistakes Grammar Bites Volume XVIII: "Words Difficult to Pronounce" and "Could Not Care Less"*

*No Mistakes Grammar Bites Volume XIX, "Punctuation" and "When You Don't Need the Word Personal"*

*No Mistakes Grammar Bites, Volume XX, "When Is Currently Needed?" And "Intervene and Interfere"*

*No Mistakes Grammar Bites, Volume XXI: "More Hyphen Questions" and Myself, Me, Themselves and Themselves."*

*No Mistakes Grammar Bites, Volume XXII: "Words You May Be Using Wrong, Part One"*

*No Mistakes Grammar Bites, Volume XXIII: "Words You May Be Using Wong, Part II"*

*No Mistakes Grammar Bites, Volume XXIV: "If and Whether," and "Incredible"*

*No Mistakes Grammar Bites, Volume XXV: "Use or Utilize" and "Dilemma"*

*No Mistakes Grammar Bites, Volume XXVI: "Alternate and Alternative" and "Plethora"*

## Writing

*No Mistakes Writing, Volume I: Writing Shortcuts*

*No Mistakes Writing, Volume II: How to Write a Bestseller*

*No Mistakes Writing, Volume III: Editing Made Easy*

*No Mistakes Writing, Volume IV: Writing Rules for Writers Who Don't Like Rules* (coming soon)

## Publishing

*How to Publish an eBook, No Mistakes Publishing, Volume I*

*How to Format an eBook, No Mistakes Publishing, Volume II*

*eBook Distribution, No Mistakes Publishing, Volume III*

*Print on Demand—Who to Use to Print Your Books, No Mistakes Publishing, Volume IV*

## Other Nonfiction

*Uneducated*

*Whiskers and Bear, Volume I, Sanctuary Tales*

*A Collection of Animal Stories, Volume II, Sanctuary Tales*

*More Animal Stories, Volume III, Sanctuary Tales*

*Surviving a Stroke—Or Two*

*Life and Then Some*

## Fiction

### Friendship & Honor Series

*Murder Takes Time*

*Murder Has Consequences*

*Murder Takes Patience*

*Murder Is Invisible*

*Murder Is a Promise*

*Murder Is Immaculate (coming soon)*

### Blood Flows South Series

*A Bullet for Carlos: A Connie Gianelli Mystery*

*Finding Family, a Novella*

*A Bullet from Dominic*

*The Good Book*

*The Ranger*

### Redemption Series

*Necessary Decisions: A Gino Cataldi Mystery*

*Old Wounds*

*Promises Kept, the Story of Number Two*

*Premeditated*

*The Ranger*

**Rules of Vengeance Series (Fantasy)**

*Light of Lights (the beginning, a novella)*

*A Promise of Vengeance*

*Undeniable Vengeance*

*Consummate Vengeance*

*Vengeance Is Mine (2019)*

**Note:** *Light of Lights* is a novella. It's about 100 pages long and sets the stage for the series. The other books in the series are between 650 and 850 pages long.

### Other Books

You can always see current and upcoming books on my website.

**Fiction**

*Memories for Sale* (mystery/sf)

*The Joshua Citadel* (SF novella)

**Children's Books**

*No Mistakes Grammar for Kids, Volume I: Much and Many*

*No Mistakes Grammar for Kids, Volume II: Lie and Lay*

*No Mistakes Grammar for Kids, Volume III:* Bring and Take

*No Mistakes Grammar for Kids, Volume IV: "Would've, Should've" and "Your and You're"*

*No Mistakes Grammar for Kids, Volume V: "There, They're, and Their" and "To, Too, and Two"*

*Shinobi Goes to School—Life on the Farm for Kids, Volume I*

*Fiona Gets Caught, Life on the Farm for Kids, Volume II*

*Coco Gets a Donut, Life on the Farm for Kids, Volume III*

*Squeak Gets a Home, Life on the Farm for Kids, Volume IV*

*Biscotti Saves Punch, Life on the Farm for Kids, Volume V*

*The Adventures of Adalina, Volume I: Adalina and the Five Tiny Bears*

**Coming Soon**

*The Adventures of Adalina, Volume II: Adalina and the Underwater Bears*

Get on the mailing list, and you'll be notified of release dates and sales.

***And don't forget to leave a review!***

Mailing list